# Craft Vinyl Decorating Ideas Gifts Home Decor and Money Making Tips Galore

## How to Master Your Cricut Machine

Maryann Gillespie

# Table of Contents

Introduction

Chapter One - Vinyl Basics ................................................. 1

Chapter Two - Choosing the Right Type of Vinyl for Your Craft Project ....................................................... 16

Chapter Three - Tips for Cutting Vinyl on Your Cricut Machine............................................................. 20

Chapter Four - Wall Art Made Simple ............................. 23

Chapter Five - Glass Etching Do's and Don'ts................ 28

Chapter Six - Stenciling Like a Pro ................................. 34

Chapter Seven - Decorating Clothing With Heat Transfer Vinyl ................................................................. 40

Chapter Eight - Best Beginner Projects ............................ 44

Chapter Nine - How Too Kiss Your Cricut Cartridges Goodbye............................................................... 47

Chapter Ten - Affordable Decorating Ideas Galore.......... 50

Chapter Eleven - Personalized Gifts for Everyone on Your List....................................................................... 62

Chapter Twelve - Money Making Ideas ........................... 71

Chapter Thirteen - 101 Inspirational Wallies.................... 85

Chapter Fourteen - Video Tutorials ................................. 91

Chapter Fifteen - FAQ'S.................................................. 93

About the Author ............................................................ 101

# Introduction

If you own a die cut machine you know one of the most popular things to cut is vinyl. It's pretty easy to work with its loads of fun and it sticks to almost any surface like walls, glass, metal, wood, stone, cloth and most plastics.

As with any other material I've used with my Cricut; there was a learning curve. I ruined a few projects before I figured it out. The reason I wrote this book was to save you some of the stress that I went through.

For newbies this guide book will provide the confidence and incentive you need to give vinyl a try. For all you experienced in the art of vinyl cutting I hope this book will open your eyes to the endless possibilities decorating with craft vinyl provides.

Whether you're looking for handmade gift ideas or you want to turn your love of crafting into a home-based business that pays for your supplies and puts a little cash in your wallet I'm here to help.

By the time you're finished reading this book you should have the knowledge to enjoy making vinyl projects with your Cricut cutter -- minus the stress.

If you want the ultimate troubleshooting guide to help you master your Cricut machine check out my first Cricut Tips book.

This is going to be fun; so let's get started!

# Chapter One - Vinyl Basics

In this chapter we're going to cover the basics of working with vinyl using your Cricut machine.

With the mass production of plastic in the 1940s it seems to have permeated our lives. We use it at home, in the workplace, at school and when having fun creating beautiful craft projects.

The type of plastic we are interested in is made up of a chemical soup with the main ingredient being Polyvinyl Chloride the same stuff PVC pipes are made of. The finished product is a thin film, soft and pliable and goes by the common name of vinyl.

When working with vinyl you'll see the terms cast and calendered which refers to the way it was made. No need to bore you with the technical details but there are some important differences. Cast vinyl is more expensive, designed for long term applications and is considered a high performance vinyl. Whereas calendered vinyl is relatively expensive and is perfect for your Cricut craft projects.

It seems that Oracal has cornered the market when it comes to craft vinyl it's what you usually find in craft stores and comes in sizes to fit most die cutters like the Cricut, Pazzles and Silhouette.

You may be familiar with Cricut vinyl (Oracal 631) which has a matte finish and works well on walls and (Oracal 651) with a glossy finish that holds up well when used outdoors. After reading this book you'll be introduced to a ton of different styles of vinyl that your Cricut machine will be able to cut.

We've all seen those consumer guides that gather information on products and serves it up to the interested public, after all an informed shopper is a smart shopper, so consider this your consumer guide to vinyl.

When you're searching websites or catalogs looking to buy vinyl you'll come across these common terms, now you'll know what they mean.

**Adhesive or craft vinyl**. Sometimes referred to as film is available in a wide variety of colors and thicknesses is weather resistant and comes backed with a removable or permanent adhesive.

**Application fluid**. The solution used in wet applications. Professional sign makers use commercial brands like RapidTac but you can make your own by mixing a couple of drops of liquid dish soap and water in a squirt bottle. The soap breaks the surface tension of the water allowing the vinyl to float on top so you can move it.

**Backing paper or release liner**. This is the paper the vinyl is stuck too. Don't ever remove this when you put the vinyl on your cutting mat.

**Carrier Sheet.** It's the backing paper of heat transfer vinyl and uses a pressure sensitive adhesive. It also acts like transfer tape to keep the vinyl in place until you apply it.

**Heat transfer, iron on or T-shirt vinyl.** This is softer than craft vinyl so it's comfortable when worn on clothing and comes backed with a heat activated adhesive. Make sure the brand you buy can be applied with a household iron. There are commercial brands that require a heat press machine and your home iron won't do the job, your design will lift or peel especially after it's been washed.

**Layering.** Is a familiar term to Cricut users and refers to stacking either different kinds or colors of vinyl on top of each other to create your design.

**Removable and permanent adhesives**. These terms do not apply to the properties of the adhesive but rather to the sticky residue left behind once you remove the vinyl. Removable adhesives like the one used on Oracal 631 leaves little if any residue behind whereas permanent adhesives Oracal 651 can cause damage when removed if left on for a long period of time (more than 3 years) because of the strong bond time creates. So removable does not mean you can peel it off and restick it over and over again nor does permanent mean it will never peel, curl or come off.

**Squeegee, scrapper or application tool.** Used to apply vinyl and smooth out air bubbles. You can use your Cricut scrapper or any plastic card with a sharp edge to burnish the vinyl to the project surface and make it stick.

**Static cling or window film.** This type of vinyl does not have an adhesive backing; instead it relies on static electricity to stick to glass, metal and plastic.

**Substrate.** Is the project surface the final resting place for your vinyl design, the surface you are applying it to whether it's a wall, glass, wood, metal or plastic.

**Transfer or application tape**. This is what you use to move your cut out vinyl letters or designs to the application surface. It comes in different styles and sizes and is either clear or opaque.

**Weeding**. Is what you do after you cut the vinyl to remove all the unwanted, excess vinyl pieces revealing the design.

**Weeding tool**. You can use a Cricut pick, X-Acto knife, needle nose tweezers, dental picks or a vinyl weeding tool there are a bunch to choose from. Here's a tip save your X-Acto blades when they get dull and won't cut anymore and turn your knife into a weeding tool.

There are a few tools besides your Cricut machine you'll need when working with vinyl. These include:

Some sort of tool to burnish the vinyl to the final surface. This can be an application tool, squeegee, craft stick or simply an old gift. It assures you get all the bubbles and creases out and the vinyl and securely attaches it to your projects surface. It's also called a burnishing tool.

A scraper or spatula to help you carefully pull up the vinyl designs without tearing them. Tweezers always come in handy. A pair of sharp scissor with pointed ends. Transfer tape which we'll talk about shortly a weeding tool and a craft knife.

Cricut cartridges, Design Studio, Gypsy or the Cricut Craft room with the designs you want to access.

Because craft vinyl is so versatile enabling you to create endless decorative objects its worth spending a little time discussing its many uses. We'll touch on just a few basic ideas in this chapter to get your creative juices flowing and help you realize the many types of projects that are possible especially if working with vinyl is new to you. In future chapters we'll discuss specific types of projects in more detail.

For a child's room or nursery the ideas are endless. You can do animals, toys or even just brightly colored shapes. Put their favorite cartoon characters on their wall or crib.

Teach preschoolers how to count, learn their ABC's or recognize colors with the help of vinyl decorations.

Lettering is another versatile use for craft vinyl. Even teenagers enjoy having their name on their wall, laptop or cell phone case.

You may want to advertise your business on your vehicle. You can create a magnetic sign or apply the lettering using exterior vinyl on the side of your car or truck. Or you can use vinyl on the inside or outside of your vehicle's windows. Exterior vinyl is recommended for outdoor projects since it has a stronger adhesive and is more resistant to UV rays.

Other uses for vinyl include personalizing wine bottles and glasses for anniversaries, parties or special occasions.

Glass kitchenware is another popular project. You can do flowers or decorative symbols or put the name of what the container holds such as Chips, Flour, Coffee, Sugar or Cookies.

You can take ordinary glass candle holders and turn them into unique decorations or personalized gifts.

You can combine vinyl decals with painted stenciled designs surrounded in an etched border for an over the top glass plague showing off the techniques you learned here.

If you have worked with vinyl and are looking for inspiration and new ideas then chapter 10 on decorating DIY projects should keep you busy.

**How to Apply Vinyl**

There are several techniques used to apply vinyl. We'll discuss 3 popular application methods.

The first is the **direct method**. Cut and weed the image then simply remove the backing paper position your design where you want it and stick it down just like you do when working with stickers. This method works best for simple images where you can just eye ball it.

When working with words or more complicated applications you'll need to understand transfer tape and how to use it for your projects. The tape keeps your cut outs in position and lets you transfer or move them safely.

There are different types of transfer tapes; paper and clear. Paper tape is more pliable and less expensive than clear tape and is a better choice if you are going to do a lot of wet applications but it's harder to see thru. The biggest advantage of clear tape is visibility you can see thru it and know exactly where your image is going.

Unlike vinyl you can reuse transfer tape a few times which keeps the cost down. Just lightly stick it to the wall or on the back of the door in your craft room.

Though transfer tape designed for this purpose works best; in a pinch you can also try masking tape or clear contact paper. The contact paper is sometimes too sticky and won't release the vinyl so you'll have to be very careful when removing it from the image. Blue painters tape can also be used.

After the vinyl has gone through your Cricut and the cuts have been made remove it from the mat. If you used a full sheet of vinyl cut around the image with scissors to make it easier to work with. Now you're ready to weed or remove all the negative (not part of the image) bits of vinyl first before you cover it with transfer tape.

This is where your weeding tool comes in handy. Use it to pick out the pieces of vinyl you don't want revealing the image you do want. Now you are ready to cover your image with transfer tape. Depending on the size of your tape you may have to overlap it to cover the entire image. Watch out for wrinkles in the tape they can cause the vinyl to wrinkle. Use the squeegee and go back and forth over the vinyl letters or image making sure you rub the image well so it attaches to the transfer tape.

At this point you have 3 layers the tape, vinyl and backing paper all in 1 easy to work with bundle. Pick it up and move it to the project you're creating and get an idea of where you want it to go making sure it fits.

Now it's time to remove the paper backing. Start in a corner and peel it back over itself at a 45 degree angle if the vinyl won't release you'll need to burnish it again until it's free. Then pick up the 2 remaining layers and place it carefully on the surface of the project right where you want it. Lay it down carefully because it's hard to correct once it adheres.

Then use a burnishing or application tool rub the image onto the surface. Make sure all air bubbles are out of the vinyl. Pull the tape off, very slowly, at a 45 degree angle. When necessary, stop and rub the vinyl again or push it down with your finger. The secret to this part is PATIENCE.

If you try to remove the tape quickly you'll probably tear a piece of the vinyl. This is especially true of intricate, delicate designs.

Here's a tip for those pesky designs that just won't stick. Wait a few minutes to let the adhesive really grab hold of the substrate. Then removing the tape should be easier.

Now we will talk about the **hinge method** the preferred way of applying wall quotes or large images. There is the horizontal hinge across the top of the graphic or the vertical hinge down the center of the graphic. Choose the one that will fit your image. You can also use this method for craft projects that require exact placement but for now I'll explain how to apply letters to walls.

Cut, weed and apply transfer tape to the letters. Now move the three layered bundle to the wall and lightly tack it in place with a couple of pieces of masking tape. Using a level make sure the letters are straight don't measure from the edge of the paper incase its not straight **measure from the letters themselves**. If you need to make adjustments just loosen the tape. When everything is level put a long piece of tape on the top edge of the paper this will act like a hinge allowing you to flip flop the vinyl. Flip the vinyl up against the wall and peel off the paper backing at an angle and cutting it with scissors if it's in the way then carefully lower the letters, pressing from top to bottom smoothing them out as you lower them to the wall. Use your burnishing tool and really rub the vinyl onto the surface smoothing out any air bubbles you see if they persist pop them with a pin and flatten them out.

If your saying has several words and it's too difficult to work with in one piece cut between the words after you have applied the hinge and flip flop each word rather than the whole sentence. The last step is to remove the transfer tape at a 45 degree angle then step back and admire your handy work, well done!

Here's an important tip to remember try to **weed your vinyl soon after cutting it**. With some brands if you set it aside and do other things it makes it harder to weed the longer you wait.

For a non-porous surface such as glass, metal or a mirror the **wet method** works well especially if it's a large image. The application fluid lets the image float allowing you to reposition it. With this method you'll need:

A ruler or straight edge
A dry erase marker
Squirt bottle with water and a few drops of dishwashing soap
Scissors
Burnishing tool
Cloth
Masking tape

First, clean your surface and let dry. You can use a glass cleaner but vinegar mixed with water works best.

You can eye ball the placement or mark off where you want to place the design with dry erase markers.

You can use the direct method or hinge method depending on the size and complexity of the decal or whichever method you prefer.

Cut, weed and apply transfer tape. Wet the surface of your project. If you are working with a large image you may want to mist the adhesive layer of the design after you removed the backing as well. Use your squirt bottle and application fluid to simply mist the surfaces. Don't over wet them.

Then lay the project down on your surface reposition if necessary.

Use your squeegee to push out all the water and air bubbles. Have your cloth on hand to wipe away the water. Make sure you get all the water out. Pull firmly with your burnishing tool but make sure you don't gouge so deeply that you move or harm the vinyl.

Take your time and make sure all the water is out. Then let the project sit for at least an hour; preferably overnight.

Finally, take a corner of the transfer tape and slowly pull it off the project. The longer it's had to dry the better because the water affects the glue and you need to give it time to set up. Take your time and pull the tape off as slowly as necessary to assure the vinyl is left in place.

If you're working with **reflective or metallic vinyl** do not use the wet method. The special properties of these films require a dry application.

## Layering Vinyl

Another unique way of using vinyl is called layering. This means using a slightly larger image of one color vinyl and then placing a small image of a different color on top. This makes a shadow effect.

Other layering uses are adding specific details to projects. In other words, you cut out the basic shape of a house in one color and then use other colors to accent windows, doors, and other details.

When applying vinyl layers just work from the background to the foreground building the image one layer at a time until you get the effect you're looking for.

If you have created greeting cards or scrapbook pages using your Cricut machine you are probably familiar with this technique.

Vinyl can be bought in many colors. You can make your projects in any color that matches your décor. It also comes in different patterns such as flowers, stripes, plaid, wood grain and animal prints.

Sometimes you can't find the perfect vinyl color but using the layering technique gives you additional options.

You can also emboss vinyl for a real cool effect. Cut it first then run it thru your embossing machine. The backing paper also gets embossed and instead of throwing it away you may like the look and find a crafty use for it.

## How to remove vinyl from car windows, car doors and walls

At some point you may get tired of your vinyl projects and want to remove them without damaging the surface they're placed on and without leaving residue behind.

For car windows, long term UV exposure will cause the vinyl to chip off in little pieces making it harder to remove. If you can park the car in the sun and heat up the vinyl you may be able to peal it off with your hands. If you're in an area that is currently cold; use a blow dryer to heat the vinyl because it removes easier when it's warm.

Use a window scraper or razor blade to scrape off harder spots.

It will leave a small amount of residue. Simply spray on some Windex let it set a few seconds, and then wipe it off with a lint free cloth. The more glue left behind, the more applications of Windex you may need to use.

For car doors heat up the vinyl and try to peel it off using a plastic razor blade to protect your paint job.

There are a lot of glue removal products you can use to clean up gummy residue like Goo-Gone and Bug and Tar Remover which won't harm the paint. Just a side note if your decal has been on for a long time and you remove it you may still see a ghost image where the vinyl was.

On a painted wall the method of removal is similar but you have to be careful to keep from damaging the surface and removing paint. It's best to remove vinyl within the first year or two.

Depending on the length of time your decals have been on the wall will determine how easy or hard they are to remove.

Generally speaking if it has been less than three years you should have no problem removing them any longer than that may require a little more effort and you may experience some surface damage.

Simply start on a corner or edge of the letter and peel it back at an angle to the wall instead of peeling straight up which could lift the paint. Just use your fingernail or tweezers to get started.

A hair dryer set on low and cool can be used to soften the vinyl do not use a heat gun. Heat the vinyl so it's warm to the touch and it should soften the adhesive enough to let your remove it. The trick is to not heat the vinyl too much as this will cause the adhesive to melt and bond even move to the wall making it harder to remove. Move the dryer back and forth a couple of inches from the wall doing a couple of letters at a time.

Some adhesive residue may be left behind on the wall. If you can't roll it off with your fingers try using masking tape to dab the wall to remove the glue.

If it still remains household cleaners can be sprayed on the wall. It's very important to test any solution you use first to see how it will affect the paint.

Rubbing alcohol will remove adhesives from wood paneling and vinyl wall coverings BUT it will dull latex paint so test first on a part of the wall that is out of sight like behind the couch.

For vinyl that has been on the walls for many years try ammonia, a little nail polish remover or Methyl Hydrate which is a form of alcohol.

If all else fails you can use turpentine, paint thinner or lightly sand the glue off the walls and repaint.

In the next chapter we'll discuss the different types of vinyl and which are best for specific projects.

# Chapter Two - Choosing the Right Type of Vinyl for Your Craft Project

Let's keep things simple. There are basically 3 kinds of vinyl, adhesive backed, static cling and heat transfer vinyl. But within these 3 types are an almost endless variety of decorative styles.

When buying vinyl you have a multitude of choices. The type you choose will depend on the project you're working on.

Here is a list of some of the more popular varieties, some of which you may be familiar with others may surprise you. When I did the research for this book I was amazed at all the really cool vinyl on the market like…

Chalk Board
Dry Erase White Board
Faux Leather
Flocked
Fluorescent
Frosted
Glitter
Glow In the Dark
Heat Transfer
Inkjet Printable
Magnetic
Metallic
Paintable Magnetic
Pre-printed patterns like wood grain, animal prints, marble and granite just to mention a few

Reflective
Rhinestone
Stained Glass
Static Cling Film
Textured
Translucent
3-D Holographic

From now on adhesive backed vinyl will be referred to as craft vinyl or Cricut vinyl. When trying to figure out which vinyl is right for your next project keep these tips in mind.

Craft vinyl is often classified as indoor or outdoor. It's taking the guess work out and telling you how to use it to achieve the best results.

Two of the most popular are Oracal 631 and Oracal 651. The 631 is considered an indoor vinyl and the 651 is for outdoor use. However, both the 631 and 651 can be used for inside or outside projects. Sign vinyl is normally used for outside projects such as on a mailbox or the outside of a vehicle. The adhesive is stronger and won't come lose in the elements as quickly.

Oracal 751, 851 and 951 are considered high performance exterior vinyl and are expected to last up to twelve years their made to resist water and UV rays but are expensive and a bit of an over kill for crafters.

So you're telling me I can't use interior vinyl outside, right? Wrong, you can. The thing to keep in mind is it will not last as long or hold up as well as exterior vinyl. It will crack, fade and peel quicker.

With that said feel free to use your outdoor vinyl to decorate your home decor items like glass, wood or plastic, with one exception. **Do not use it** for wall quotes or sayings as the strong adhesive could literally pull the paint or plaster right off the wall when removed.

Sample packs - This is a good way to buy several types of vinyl at a reasonable price so you can try them out.

Keep in mind that these packs sometimes contain vinyl of different thicknesses. So just when you think you have the settings perfect, you discover the new sheet of vinyl you're working with is slightly thicker or thinner which may require an adjustment in depth.

**Saving money on vinyl**

Be sure and do a little surfing online for the best vinyl prices. Sometimes Amazon, eBay or other craft sites offer cheaper prices than the Cricut store. But make sure you're comparing the same types of vinyl.

Here are some other sites that offer craft vinyl at discount prices.

expressionsvinyl.com
craftvinyl.com
myvinyldirect.com
cricutdiecuttingmachine.com

Vinyl comes in sheets or rolls. You can often save money by buying in rolls which are usually 24" wide and need to be cut to fit your machine. Ask the seller if he will cut it for you.

If there is a sign shop close by maybe you can buy your rolls from him since he buys in bulk he may be willing to give you a good price. Before you purchase an entire roll; try to test the type of vinyl using a single piece. You don't want to be stuck with a large roll that doesn't work well for your projects.

Not every Cricut crafter uses enough vinyl to warrant buying rolls so ask your local sign shops if they are willing to sell you the vinyl scraps they have from large projects.

## Chapter Three - Tips for Cutting Vinyl on Your Cricut Machine

This is often the tricky part. When you first start working with vinyl you'll probably ruin a few sheets with cuts that are too deep -- and cut into the backing -- or too shallow and won't lift off without tearing.

I'm going to tell you the settings that I use for craft vinyl. However, you may need to adjust if you're working with thicker sheets or different types of vinyl.

The secret to cutting most vinyl projects is to not cut through the backing. This is called a "kiss cut". It barely grazes the top of the vinyl cutting through the film layer but not the paper backing.

This isn't always true, though. If you're cutting a stencil you may choose to cut all the way through the vinyl and the backing. But we'll talk about that more in a future chapter.

Put you vinyl paper side down on the mat and use these settings.

I set my blade depth on 3
Pressure at 3
And speed at 3

For thicker types of vinyl you may need to adjust the settings slightly. These are just the ones I've found work best for me. Each brand of vinyl is different. Start with the settings I suggested and then make slight changes until you find the perfect cut for your machine.

Cutting vinyl can be tricky for several reasons like the age of the vinyl, is the blade dull or dirty and the condition of the mat. The thickness of the vinyl is also a factor as well as the brand. Use small test cuts so you don't waste a lot of vinyl if you're having problems.

Vinyl scraps from sign companies are sometimes **thicker than craft vinyl** so you'll need to adjust for deeper cuts.

If the vinyl refuses to cut well and the backing is coming loose the vinyl may be old. Return it to the retailer for a refund.

Use the paper saver button to conserve vinyl or move your blade to make your cuts near the edges and sides of the sheets. This will allow you to use the rest of the vinyl sheet on another project.

Try to keep the blade free from debris. Sometimes just cleaning the blades will correct cutting problems especially if you have adhesive buildup on the tip from cutting vinyl. This is also true of the mat. If you have fibers stuck to the mat from another project it will hinder getting accurate cuts on new projects.

If you're still having problems cutting your vinyl it might be time to replace the blade in your Cricut. Try adjusting your pressure and depth first, if that doesn't work try new blades.

If the vinyl is moving while being cut use a new mat or restick the old one. There can also be a problem if your mat has deep cut marks in it from previous projects.

Another problem that results in poor cuts is using cheap unknown brands. If you continue to have problems try the Cricut vinyl (Oracal) and see if you get better results.

I always try to store my vinyl in plastic containers unless I'm using it quickly. This protects it from dust or lint settling on the vinyl and interfering with the cutting process.

I also prefer to store vinyl in flat sheets. Some vinyl rolls will lay flat when unrolled and other tend to maintain the rounded form. This makes cutting difficult.

For this reason I wouldn't suggest storing rolls for long periods of time without use. You can always go ahead and cut mat size squares so they'll be ready for immediate use and you can store them flat. Again, with some rolls this isn't necessary.

I never store vinyl for more than two years after that is can start to lose its flexibility. Also, the adhesive will start to lose strength.

# Chapter Four - Wall Art Made Simple

Wall art is an inexpensive way to decorate your home or office and offers a variety of options for any living space limited only by your imagination. It can add a visual impact to any room at a fraction of the cost of framed art.

You can use designs such as flowers, trees, animals, abstract designs and patterns, geometric shapes any image you want from your cartridges.

Or you can use a quote or an inspirational saying that expresses your thoughts. (See chapter 13 for over 100 wall quotes you can use for inspiration.)

Kitchen decals are also popular. These include:
Fruit and vegetable shapes
Wine bottles
Tea cups and tea pots
Butterflies
Flowers
Types of food like pies or cookies
There are a multitude of different options for children's rooms which include:
Animals
Cartoon figures
Sports teams
School logos or mascots
Kid's names
Quotes
Murals

Super heroes

Peace signs

Names of popular bands or TV and movie stars

A lot of these designs will also work well for a dorm room when a student doesn't have a big decorating budget. Or if you're an apartment dweller and your landlord won't let you hang pictures on the wall.

Most people use a craft vinyl with a matte finish for wall quotes because it looks like custom hand painted lettering. But if you want more than plain black letters try patterned, metallic, textured or glitter vinyl for your letters and layer them to get that WOW effect.

When working with letters keep this in mind, **the bolder the font the smaller the size you can choose**. The real delicate scripts rip and stretch and are harder to work with. To get the best results keep your letters at least 1/2" and not less than 1/3" when cutting vinyl letters. Did you know that many image cartridges also include fonts so you don't have to buy font cartridges unless you want too?

It is not necessary to weld your letters together unless that is the look you want, like with cursive script cartridges. Using transfer tape will keep your letters straight and in place until you apply them. In case you're not familiar with the term welding is when you connect the letters together so they all cut out in one piece. Some cartridges have words or sayings already welded but for the most part you have to do it yourself. You can use the Gypsy, Design Studio software or the Cricut Craft room to weld letters together.

## Prepping your walls to avoid problem applications

Never apply vinyl to newly painted walls. Wait at least 3-4 weeks to allow the paint to cure and the gasses to escape or your decals will be filled with bubbles. It's not unusual to see bubbles crop up weeks after your installation just smooth them out or pop them with a pin and eventually they will go away.

It's also vital that you clean your wall and remove all dirt, grease or smoke build up. Inspect the wall to see if there are any dents, gouges, peeling or chipped paint as these will cause trouble.

If you have applied the vinyl correctly and no matter what you do it just won't stick to the wall it may not be your fault. Some premium paints have additives to make them stain resistant which interfere with the glue. Also vinyl will not stick to some types of glazes and satin finish and flat matte paint may also cause you trouble.

To avoid frustration do not apply vinyl lettering to these surfaces as well which include brick, cinder block, concrete, heavily textured, leather, oxidized peeling paint, plaster, stucco, wood paneling, raw wood, unpainted metal and wallpaper.

Applying vinyl wall decals is not complicated. Here are the step by step directions to make the process as simple as possible.

Choose the design you want to use on your Cricut. If you're doing a quote you'll probably have to cut the words in several sections rather than one long sentence. Make sure you use the same font and size for each word.

Cut the vinyl using a "kiss cut". You want the vinyl cut but not the backing.

Remove or weed the negative pieces from your cut sheet of vinyl. Apply transfer tape to the lettering. Clean and dry the wall surface.

Make light marks with pencil on the wall so you're sure your design will be placed in exactly the right spot. You want it to be level and centered correctly (remember measure from the letters not the edge of the paper). Some people prefer to use a level rather than eye balling it to assure the art is level. This is usually more important with lettering than just a single image.

Use the hinge method discussed in chapter 1 securing the transfer tape with your letters and backing paper to the wall. Cut between the words making it easier to work with if necessary.

Flip the letters up and remove the backing on an angle. Flop them down and use an application tool to adhere the vinyl to the wall smoothing out all the bubbles.

Remove transfer tape slowly and carefully at a 45 degree angle. If the vinyl letters starts to come off, then use the application tool again. Erase any placement marks you made.

Note: If vinyl lettering is removed within the first couple of years it should remove easily. After three years it will often leave a residue on the wall or damage the paint.

When you become an expert at installing vinyl lettering on walls why not offer that service as a gift. Just create the saying or inspirational quote and install it on your friends wall. Or better yet start your own vinyl lettering business.

I have included short video tutorials with step by step instructions. See chapter 14 for added help.

# Chapter Five - Glass Etching Do's and Don'ts

I've enjoyed many of the projects I do with vinyl. One of my favorites is glass etching. With this technique you can make exquisite personalized gifts and fabulous home accents.

I recently made a set of wine glasses for my niece and nephew who were getting married. I stenciled each of their names on the glasses using the method I'm about to tell you. They used the glasses at their wedding reception.

In a later chapter we're going to talk about ways you can make money selling your vinyl crafts. Personalized glass etchings are one of the best products to sell.

For glass etching you'll be cutting out a stencil for the design you want.

I like to use the Storybook cartridge for lettering but you can use any design you choose that fits on the glass container you're etching. Be careful about pulling the stencil around curves or corners. This can sometimes make the stencil bubble or distort the design. We'll talk about this more later. The point is to use smaller designs when possible.

I use a blade depth of 3
Pressure at 3
And speed at 3

As with all settings; you may need to adjust based on the thickness of vinyl you're using to make a "kiss cut".

Then remove the letters to leave a negative. In other words, if you're printing the name SUSAN you don't want to leave the letters on the stencil. You want the empty space to say Susan.

If you like the look of frosted glass try reversing the method and use a positive image. You would apply the letters SUSAN and cover the entire surface with the etching cream. The only part of the glass that would be clear is the letters.

Make sure to leave enough of a vinyl border when you trim your design so that you can apply the cream and not go over the edge on to the glass you don't want etched.

Clean the surface of the glass with alcohol and dry with a soft cloth. Make sure to wipe off your fingerprints as the oil from your skin can interfere with the etching process.

Remove the backing paper and place the stencil on the glass using the direct method if the design is small or you may want to use the hinge method and transfer tape for larger or complex designs.

Continue to apply pressure until all the air bubbles are out and the vinyl adheres to the glass. This can be trickier on glasses or anything where the design is on a rounded surface. Be patient and apply pressure carefully. You don't want the vinyl to move, but it must be firmly applied. If any edges are not secure the cream will seep onto unwanted surfaces and ruin your design.

The best way to attach a stencil to a rounded surface is to start in the middle and work toward the edges. Cut slits in the vinyl so the stencil has some leeway for the curve of the glass. If the slits in the vinyl pull apart you should cover them with tape. This will keep the area from getting etched accidently.

If the vinyl refuses to stick to the rounded edges you may need to use a smaller design or font size. It's usually best to try a flat surface for your first etching project. This can be a baking dish or a squared cubed candle holder or even a mirror.

Once the stencil is applied you'll use etching cream such as Armour Etch or Etchall. Martha Stewart also sells an etching cream. I have used Armour Etch with success but some people have complained it can sometimes be blotchy. So you might want to compare different creams to see which one works best for you. I'll talk about the different creams at the end of the chapter.

Use a soft brush, craft stick or a Q-tip to carefully dab on the etching cream. Be careful that the etching cream doesn't touch any parts of your project that you do not want etched. If it does, remove it with a soft cloth as quickly as possible.

Since these products are a type of acid; it's a good idea to use gloves when working with etching fluid of any kind. Be very careful not to rub your eyes and try to keep the cream off your skin as much as possible. Wash it off quickly when you do get some on your skin. Always work in a well-ventilated area.

Let it set according to the directions of the product you're using some need to set a longer time to etch properly while others will start to eat the stencil if left too long.

Then rinse off with cold water. Or if your product is reusable scrape off the cream and put it back in the bottle and then rinse it off.

**Save your sink and the environment**

Note: Etching cream can harm sinks and counter tops so be very careful as you rinse it off. Rinse of the etching cream into a plastic bowel or tub and add a heaping handful of baking soda to the water to neutralize the acid before you dump it down the drain.

Removing the stencil from the glass when wet is easier. As the glass dries the image will get darker. Stand back and admire your handy work!

**Reusable glass etching stencils**

If you have dozens of glasses to monogram you might want to invest in precut reusable stencils. They don't last forever but might be an effective alternative.

I have heard of Cricut crafters reusing their own vinyl stencils by just letting them air dry a day or two before reusing them the next time.

Shelf liner seems to be a reusable stencil material. The adhesive will stick over and over again even after getting wet.

**The three most popular etching creams are:**

**Armour Etch** - This has been the standard etching cream I've used for years. The smell is strong so always use in a well-ventilated area. It does sometimes have lumps that cause blotchy results. I usually leave it on for twenty minutes which is longer than the recommended time. (See the video tutorial section for a way to get rid of the blotchy results.)

**Etchall** - One big advantage this etching cream has is you can return unused portions to the jar to reuse. Which means there is less waste and makes this cream slightly more affordable.

**Martha Stewarts Etching Cream** - This is more expensive than the other etching creams but tends to be less blotchy. Also, the smell is not as overwhelming. It might be worth paying a little more if your budget allows.

For more of a professional grade etching cream try:

McKay Velvet Etching Cream
Vari-Etch
Matronics Professional 30 Second Formula

Not a big fan of etching cream but like the look of etched glass? Well now you can get that same look in a can of spray paint. It gives glass and mirrors the frosted look of etched glass without using acid creams. Just do a search for frosted or etched glass spray paint to find products by **Krylon, Rust-Oleum and Valspar**.

Here's a **money saving tip** for all of us who recycle and have a supply of glass bottles and jars. If you're new to etching or you want to experiment just use the glass in your recycling bins to practice on.

Once I was confident I headed to the dollar store and checked out garage sales to see what ideas I could come up with for etching projects. I turned cheap, plain glass items into beautiful art glass with intricate patterns and created unique personalized gifts my friends still rave about.

# Chapter Six - Stenciling Like a Pro

Stenciling is a popular way to add patterns to walls, floors, furniture, clothing, glass, mirrors, fabric, paper, ceilings or almost any other object.

You can use paint, glaze, metallic powder, gold, silver or copper leaf, Gesso, plaster, joint compound or molding paste. By using stencils you can take a plain piece of furniture or a boring wall and make it a unique decorative item in your home.

You use the stencil like a pattern to help you paint a design in a decorative manner. Much like an artist would freehand it. With stencils everyone can be an artistic genius even if you can't draw.

Stencils are often made from vinyl which is why I added this chapter to the book.

Another popular stencil material is Mylar. The big difference between this polyester film and vinyl is that it does not have an adhesive backing. It is reusable, durable and resists tearing. Mylar can also be cut using your Cricut; the settings will vary depending on thickness of the sheets you buy.

When working with stencils you have options. You can remove the backing and stick the vinyl on the surface of your project or leave the backing and secure the vinyl with tape or a light spray adhesive. The advantage being your stencil is now reusable when you keep the backing paper intact. It is also easily repositioned.

With other vinyl projects you pull away the negative parts of the vinyl. In other words, if you're using a flower you weed away anything that is not the flower and then apply the flower to your project.

Stencils are, of course, just the opposite. You pull the flower part away and leave the negative space. It's the negative space that is the image of the flower that you'll fill in with paint.

When working with a reusable stencil you'll have to adjust the setting on your Cricut machine to cut all the way through the vinyl AND the backing. For a one time use stencil use the kiss cut and weed your image.

Remove your stencil from the mat. Clean the surface of the area you're going to paint and let it dry.

Apply the stencil using whatever method you choose making sure it's placed where you want it. Tape the reusable stencil securely in place you don't want it to move or if you've removed the backing make sure all the edges of the design adhere securely or paint will get under the edges.

Pat the paint on as opposed to brushing. If you brush too hard you can get paint under the stencil. You don't want paint anywhere except inside the stencil area. You can also use a foam pouncer or a foam roller. You want to apply the paint evenly but assure that none gets under the stencil. If it bleeds just lift the stencil and wipe it off.

When working with paint don't over load the brush with too much paint. You'll get better results applying two thin coats and waiting between coats for the paint to dry.

Don't think you have to use only one color of paint for each design. You can add strokes of different colors or blend them for a shaded look.

Use touches of white paint along the top of designs to give the appearance of highlighting.

Use a touch of dark paint to achieve a look of depth or a 3D shadow effect.

When making a continuing pattern always use at least three or four of the designs in a row. This way you can overlap the last shape and make sure the pattern is even with the same amount of distance between each shape.

**Relief stenciling**

Instead of a flat design you can add dimension to simulate carved wood or plaster relief decorations on walls, ceilings or doors using joint compound or a host of other products that are easy to work with and achieve extraordinary results.

Using a mixture of Gesso and glue instead of paint will make a textured stencil that stands out from the surface in relief.

You can then sand the image carefully to make them smooth and even.

Paint can be added to the Gesso before it's used or you can paint the designs after it has completely dried.

Use glue in the stencil and then place sand on top. This makes another textured design. You can use plain sand or colored sand depending on the look you want to achieve.

**Popular stencil projects include:**

Borders on walls, these are usually at the top of the wall or in the middle of the wall acting like a chair rail. If you're stenciling walls around a corner you may need to cut a notch in the stencil so it will bend around or into the corner.

If you like the look of inlaid wood or parquetry floors but not the hefty price try stenciling a center medallion, geometric patterns or a floral border.

Adding patterns on wooden furniture can make any thrift store find look new and interesting. Chairs, tables, dressers, desks and entertainment centers can be given a whole new look.

Glass jars or decorative dishes can be stenciled. Depending on the type of paint you use they may not be suitable as dinnerware so you can't eat off them. Also, painted dishes usually are not dishwasher safe.

Turn that old glass table top into a family heirloom with reverse painting on glass the centuries old art form you can recreate with stenciling.

Reproduce the antique look of Verre Eglomise by guiding glass with metal leaf.

Create stained glass windows by stenciling using glass paint it's removable on glass and mirrors so you can change the design often.

You can stencil a "welcome mat" on a wooden porch by simply painting the stenciled design directly on the porch. It will give the impression of a mat or rug.

Stencil a design on a piece of canvas to make your own Persian rug or wall hanging.

Canvas tote bags are another project that adds value to what is originally an inexpensive, non-decorative item.

Hanging ornaments make good stenciled crafts. You can buy inexpensive ornaments and then personalize them with baby names or the names of a couple celebrating their first anniversary.

Dry or relief embossing stationary or notecards is another use for stencils. You make a cut out of the stencil design on cardboard instead of buying metal stencils. This is great way to make personalized note cards using your initials or a favorite symbol.

Custom lighting can be expensive but you can convert bottles or mason jars into instant lamps and either etch or paint designs to produce one of a kind collectables. There are several bottle or jar lamp kits to choose from.

## Create imitation porcelain

Not a big fan of spray paint? Have you seen the metallic paint that looks like shinny chrome, antique gold, hammered copper or oiled bronze?

Try using Rust-Oleum bright coat for a shiny look and Rust-Oleum metallic paint for a more classic look.

Here's how to turn any cheap glass items into expensive looking porcelain. Just use Rust-Oleum painters touch gloss paint in your favorite colors to create foux Belleek, Celadon or Delft pottery.

You can use a spray painted surface as is or add vinyl decorations for further embellishment.

Remember: When painting on a stencil it's best to dab paint on or brush gently to prevent bleeding. You want your design to have sharp clean edges. You can always practice on paper until you master the technique. With that said the charm of stenciling is that it's not perfect. It's ok if it looks a little funky.

# Chapter Seven - Decorating Clothing with Heat Transfer Vinyl

Have you ever wanted a T-shirt with a specific decal, sports team or real cute saying and couldn't find what you wanted?

Now you can make your own vinyl decorations for T-shirts, hoodies or any other cloth items.

There are different types of vinyl that can be used for clothing. Some merely use a sticky, adhesive backing that you apply directly onto the cloth. This brand does not always stay in place especially after the clothing is washed.

Iron on or heat transfer vinyl works much better. With this vinyl you apply the design to the shirt and then use an iron and pressure to activate the adhesive to attach it to the cloth.

Iron on vinyl comes in dozens of basic colors. If you looking for something special try glow in the dark, fluorescent, flocked, patterned, metallic or glitter heat transfer vinyl. You can layer iron on vinyl to create multi colored applications.

For custom images there are printable heat transfer vinyl sheets to use with your printer.

Most iron on film works best on cotton and polyester but these brands work on nylon and leather Siser EasyWeed Extra and ThermoFlex Xtra. No doubt you will find other brands that work well on specialty fabrics when you do your search.

Cricut.com has its own brand of iron-on and printable iron-on vinyl as well.

If you're in doubt as to which vinyl products to buy; spend some time reading the reviews from users. This can be enlightening as to what products meet the user's needs.

Before applying vinyl wash the item if possible. Do not use any dryer sheets or liquid fabric softener.

NOTE: When you're purchasing heat transfer vinyl make sure it's the kind that can be applied with a home iron. Some vinyl must be applied with professional heat press equipment and will never adhere with just a household iron.

## Cutting and applying T-shirt vinyl

First, choose the image you want to use on your Cricut machine. I like to cut the image out on paper first and place it on the item of clothing to see if it's the size I want. That way I don't waste vinyl.

When working with this type of vinyl you need to flip the design or mirror the image. That way it will look correctly when you iron it on. **You'll need to spell words backwards and then flip them too.** Write the words on paper so you can see how their spelled when you enter them on your Cricut.

Place the vinyl shiny side down on your mat. You only want the cut to "kiss" the vinyl it should not cut through the shiny backing. **The carrier sheet will act like transfer tape** since its clear it's easy to see where to position it. Cut and weed your image. Just so you know some heat transfer vinyl is harder to weed than regular vinyl.

When cutting iron-on vinyl these settings work well
Speed at 3
Pressure at 3
But blade at 2

Always put a piece of cloth or a Teflon sheet over the design before you iron it on. Do not place the iron directly on the vinyl or it will pucker. Do not use the steam setting on the iron.

You can pre heat the garment for a few seconds. Iron on a hard surface such as cutting board so you can apply pressure. Rather than ironing with a back and forth motion which can move the vinyl lift and press the iron straight down lifting the iron across the image. Using firm pressure will help the vinyl to adhere to the cloth.

With some vinyl you can let cool before you remove the backing while others say to remove it while it's still warm. Follow the directions that come with the product for best results especially if you have a corner that's peeling and not sticking.

When washing clothing that I've applied vinyl too; I prefer to use cold water and delicate settings. This is not completely necessary, I just find it makes the vinyl look nice for a longer period of time and helps the adhesive last longer.

T-shirts are not the only use for iron on vinyl. Here are a few other ideas:

Jackets
Hoodies
Ball caps
Quilts
Pillows
Tablecloth
Placemats
Table runners
Wall tapestries
Backpacks
Cloth tote bags
Banners
Flags

REMEMBER: You want to create a mirror image so flip your design. When applying lettering words need to be spelled backwards and flipped as well.

# Chapter Eight - Best Beginner Projects

In this chapter we're going to talk about some of the easier types of projects to start your adventure in vinyl.

Static cling vinyl or window cling film is a perfect beginner project because it has no adhesive backing. It is reusable, repositionable and you don't have to use transfer tape which makes it easier to work with for newbies. It sticks to glass, metal and plastic.

Let me point out that there is a limit to the number of times it can be repositioned. It will eventually stop sticking well. (Read the directions for your particular brand of static cling vinyl to learn how to restick it.) Generally speaking when that happens just rinse it off in water let it dry and it will stick like magic again. Save the backing paper and remount your decal when you store it.

Static cling vinyl is perfect for seasonal projects where you'll only have the vinyl displayed for a few weeks. Your kids can help you apply the designs because it's not imperative that they are placed perfectly the first time.

For first projects select larger designs that do not have a lot of intricate details. This makes weeding the project and transferring it to the substrate much easier.

Take your time and weed out the parts of the vinyl that are not part of the design. Some static cling vinyl is thinner than other vinyl films so be careful.

As you progress you'll be able to work with intricate designs but they can be frustrating for a beginner.

To sum up: Start with fairly low-cost projects so you won't be as upset if they don't turn out perfect. I also suggest starting with projects with a flat surface. Rounded surfaces increase the chances of wrinkles causing the vinyl to pucker. If that happens just peel it back and smooth it out being careful not to tear it.

Write down the settings you used. If they work perfectly then you don't have to worry about remembering them for next time. If they don't; then you can adjust accordingly and not repeat the same mistakes.

## Cheap alternatives

Not sure you're ready to use your expense vinyl yet? Try some projects with contact paper first. It's cheap and works on many surfaces.

Don't want to buy transfer tape? There are cheaper alternatives you can try. Some people use masking tape or blue painters tape. A friend says she always uses clear contact paper. I have used masking tape in an emergency when I ran out of transfer tape and it did work on small designs. Because transfer tape was specially designed for its use I feel it works better than the alternatives.

## How to reuse vinyl

One of the biggest complaints crafters have about vinyl is you can't reuse it. Once you pull it off the substrate its usually torn or stretched beyond use. Well I'm here to tell you I reuse it all the time and here's how I do it.

I use static cling vinyl as the foundation and simply stick my adhesive vinyl cut designs to it. I can make the design a single layer or build multiply layers of different colors, patterns or textures until I get the look I'm after.

When I want to change the look of things I simple remove the layered decal and replace it with a new design storing the old one for future use.

## Chapter Nine - How Too Kiss Your Cricut Cartridges Goodbye

Do you want to have an endless source of images that you can import and turn into vinyl creations without having to buy a Cricut Explore machine? I'm talking any design, image, font, pattern, art work, logo, photo, kid's drawings any digital picture you can capture is now available to you on printable vinyl.

With printable adhesive vinyl you can reproduce images on vinyl and eliminate machine cutting and weeding. You cut the designs out by hand with scissors or a craft knife.

No need to worry about getting the letters straight when applying the vinyl because you just cut the whole saying as one piece of vinyl like a sticker instead of individual letters.

Intricate patterns you could never cut on a Cricut machine are now available to you with this print and hand cut option.

There are several brands of printable vinyl on the market for both inkjet and laser printers. There is also printable cling vinyl as well like Papilio's Static and Ultra Cling vinyl. It comes in clear and white sheets that you just print on using an inkjet printer.

Here are a few things to keep in mind. Inkjet printable vinyl will only work with inkjet printers and not laser printers. Printer settings should be on best print quality to produce clean images.

Wait 10 minutes for the ink to dry before cutting unless your printer dries instantly. It will stick to the same surfaces as regular vinyl.

If the brand of inkjet vinyl you purchased is waterproof you can use it outdoors but the image will fade in sunlight. For UV protection you can use a spray laminate. For a fade resistant image the laser printable vinyl lasts longer.

The projects you can create with printable vinyl are only limited by your imagination. I'm sure once you start thinking about them you'll come up with great ideas like these.

For a child's room you can print words like toys, books, shoes or laundry and also a picture of each item for younger children who can't read yet and stick them on bins or baskets.

Within a short time they'll be able to read the words thanks to seeing them connected to the pictures! These baskets can help curb the chaos of a child's room while teaching them to put everything back in it proper place.

Kids are crazy about stickers now you can print photographic quality stickers with a desktop printer. Create your own custom sticker, decals or bumper stickers with a favorite image, sports team or photograph.

A star is borne! Copy your favorite movie poster and insert your own portrait images with the help of photo editing software.

One of the coolest things to create with printable vinyl is your miniature family. You've seen the stick figures on car windows well why not print photos of family members on printable vinyl cut them out and mount them on paper doll stands. That way you have lifelike images of your loved ones to keep you company on your desk at work, don't forget to make one of the family pet too.

**For all you artists**

If you can draw then paintable magnetic vinyl is a way to reproduce your artwork. Use markers or paint right on this white vinyl.

To sum it up you can use any digital image and reproduce it on several types of **printable adhesive, magnetic, static cling or iron on vinyl**.

# Chapter Ten - Affordable Decorating Ideas Galore

## Home décor made easy

The beauty of being able to decorate practically anything gives you the freedom to experiment and after reading this book the confidence to create unique handmade objects to decorate your home.

You'll no longer have to look for those 20% off home furnishings sales you'll be able to create the look you want and have fun doing it.

For the most part these are inexpensive items that you can embellish with vinyl letters and designs. The ease of which these items can be made lets you change your design scheme at the drop of a hat.

You'll never get tired of looking at the same old decor again. You can tweak these decorating ideas to fit almost any room in your home.

They also make great gift ideas too. Nothing says you care or "I have been thinking of you" like a gift with that special someone's name on it.

Also feel free to use any of these decorating ideas to create craft items for sale. There's a whole chapter on how to sell Cricut crafts whether you just want to make a few bucks to help pay for your craft supplies or you become the next Martha Stewart, that chapter is a good starting point.

So let's get started with these creative ideas that will inspire you to decorate your home for less.

**Kitchen**

*Update kitchen cabinets* by turning inexpensive drawer pulls into fancy looking handles. Remove the old knob and apply your vinyl decal where the old handle was then re-attach the handle centering it in the design to create a custom look.

Did you know people create *high-end looking appliances* by adding stainless steel vinyl to plain white refrigerators and dishwashers? I was shocked when I did the research and found there was actually stainless steel vinyl. Make sure you check out the video tutorial section for the how to remodel your kitchen video.

Add new life to any *counter top* with granite or marble vinyl. I didn't know this existed either I thought adhesive vinyl was just for crafting.

Now that you've remodeled your kitchen with the above suggestion don't forget the *switch plates and outlets* even small objects can make a big impact with the right touch.

Spice up your kitchen with vinyl decorations and match the design on *tea towels, pot holders and oven mitts* that hang on the oven or center island.

Now you can create your own *perpetual calendars* with dry erase whiteboard vinyl. Just draw a template and fill in the days and dates of each month.

List all your emergency numbers and contact information for each family member and make your *whiteboard* the first place everybody looks to when something unexpected happens.

Create a *family messaging center* using chalkboard vinyl. Post your schedule for the day that way everyone knows where you are. It also serves as a visual reminder and helps you keep track of appointments.

Need incentive to get all those daily chores done? Just write you're *to do list for the day* on your chalkboard and erase them once they're accomplished.

A chalk board is great in the pantry. That way you keep a *running grocery list* as you run out of something just write it down as a reminder.

Do you host themed dinner parties? Decorate *charger plates* and the *center piece* to follow the party theme.

The 99 cent store is filled with ceramic items just waiting to be decorated. The next time you have a dinner party send your guests home with a *commemorative plate* that honors the occasion.

Make going green with *cloth grocery bags* fun. Add whatever you want whether it's a money saving slogan or cute food shaped designs to the outside of the bag. Show the decorated bags to the store owner where you shop, he may hire you to customize the clothe bags he sells.

Translucent vinyl works best when decorating *wine bottle lamps* filled with battery operated LED lights that hang in trees or from you patio roof. (Check out the video tutorial chapter and learn the do's and don'ts of glass bottle cutting and how to make your own cheap glass cutting tool.)

Turn your *kitchen herb garden* and those drab *flower pots* into whimsical wonders with the aid of vinyl and trim your designs with beads, rocks, shells and mosaic tiles.

Have you seen *tole painted metal trays*? They're just gorgeous so why not create your own. You can paint the designs on using stencils or use vinyl cut outs.

Create a kitchen vignette by grouping bottles *of herb infused oils and flavored vinegars* all of which you made yourself of course in fancy bottles you etched, painted or decorated with vinyl.

Give your glass or *ceramic canister set* that designer look by decorating it with your kitchen theme. Don't forget the cookie jar and any other small kitchen appliances you may store on the counter. Instead of standing out they will blend right into you decorating scheme.

Nobody likes doing laundry so fill your *laundry room walls* with your favorite sayings that touch your heart or a poem that makes your laugh out loud that way doing chores will be less or a chore.

If you have a plain white *washer and dryer* add some color with simple geometric designs. Just cut circles, squares, triangles and hearts and use the direct application method. Just peel and stick the vinyl in place. This is a great beginner project.

*Keep yourself safe* if you jog at night or take Fido for a walk making it easy for drivers to see you. Decorate your jacket and the back of your running shoes with reflective vinyl and don't forget to put some on your furry friend's collar and leash too!

## Livingroom

Make it easier for emergency services to find your home by displaying *your house number* on a decorative plaque, ceramic tiles or on a yard sign. You can make house numbers from reflective vinyl that can be easily seen at night.

Bring a smile to the mailman's face when he delivers your mail by *customizing your mailbox*.

Don't forget your *husband's man cave* it can be decorated with his college sports teams, outdoor activities or his favorite movie.

For all of you animal lovers who want pets but not necessarily all the work that comes with them. Now you can fill your walls with *maintenance free companions*. Create a faux aquarium and fill it with exotic fish and sea creatures.

These make believe cats, kittens, dogs and puppies will always get along on your walls. No need for a cage with these feathery friends and even wild animals can decorate your home safely.

Going for that *rustic cabin look*? Then wooden blocks, plaques, trays or even sliced logs will give you ample surface to decorate.

A set of 4 x 4 ceramic tiles can be monogramed or decorated and grouped together to make *costar sets*. They make great house warming gifts too.

Glue several tiles you've embellished to decorative ribbon to create *wall hangings*.

Just visit the home improvement store or tile shop featuring *stone and decorative ceramic tiles* to find gorgeous 12 x 12 tiles to choose from. They can be decorated and framed or displayed on countertop easels. The same goes for 12 x 12 mirror tiles.

You don't have to start from scratch you can *embellish existing items* like wall clocks. Add an inspirational quote to the wall above the clock or surround the clock with seasonal designs.

*Combine vinyl lettering with physical objects* like pictures or mirrors. Put a border of words around your mirror or top each picture frame with a vinyl design or image.

Call attention to the *fireplace mantel* by adding an inspirational saying above it or surround the fireplace itself with formal or whimsical designs.

Apply vinyl words or designs to *decorative candles, glass holders, votive or candle sticks*. Some battery operated *flameless candles* are just plain white so jazz them up too.

*Sliding glass doors* pose a hazard sometimes if you forget the door is closed. Use static cling vinyl that you can change often and keep your home safe. Let your children choose the designs you apply to make your home decor lively. Since it's a simple peel and stick application they can install it too.

Wall art does not have to be famous words or poems you can also decorate with images if you are *tracing your family history* a tree with leaves representing each member of the family might be interesting.

Update the look of your *stair case* by decorating the stair risers. Either apply your designs directly for a long term application or apply them to a veneer of medium-density fiberboard (MDF), particle board or plywood for easy removal. That way you can change the look often.

If you like the idea of wall quotes but want to change them up from time to time apply lettering to *plaques or cloth banners* instead of the walls and hang them like pictures.

*Ceilings* were highly decorated in the past with murals, geometric patterns and ceiling medallions. Now you can breathe new life into this forgotten and often neglected surface by adding your own vinyl decoration as a border, in the corners or surrounding the light fixture.

If you have *lighting fixtures* like wall sconces put an attractive decoration around it perhaps with glossy or reflective vinyl and watch the shimmering effect the light has on it.

Make your own million dollar Ming Vase by turning a plain white vase into a priceless antique. Just make your own blue and white porcelain design and apply it. Get in the habit of saving pictures of *decorative art objects* you want to copy. Then look for inexpensive items that you can use to re-create the same expensive look.

Dress up your *front door* with festive door hangers or wreathes for each season of the year. Garden flags and ornamental figurines can be given a new look to brighten up your lawn or patio by adding exterior vinyl decorations.

Wondering what to do with the left over scraps of marble or granite from your newly remolded kitchen or bath? You guessed it vinylize it. Make an *outdoor sign* saying home sweet home est. 1999, please wipe your paws or attack cat on duty - using exterior vinyl and display it by the front door.

What does your door mat say about you? Pineapples have long been a symbol of hospitality; why not add them to your *welcome mat*.

Here is how to *add privacy to any glass door*, French doors or front door glass surround. We will discuss several options. There is static cling window film that is easy to apply since it has no adhesive backing. It comes in a variety of colors and patterns.

For a more permanent application there is self-adhesive window film. Again the choices are endless you can choose from frosted, etched, stained glass, translucent colors and patterns.

You can apply it directly to the window or to clear Plexiglas inserts that fit your windows and door surrounds for and easy to remove and change option.

Reproducing Tiffany like stained glass windows is a snap with this type of window film.

One of the biggest complaints people have with self-adhesive window films is they are hard to remove. For a quick solution to the problem check out the video on how to remove frosted vinyl from your windows in the video tutorial section.

**Bathroom**

Dress up your powder room with *decorative towels*, you know the ones you put out when company is coming. Iron on vinyl appliques work well for this project. To make the design stand out use a flocked vinyl it looks good with the nap of the towel. Bath mats also look extra special with a custom design.

*Hand painted porcelain thrones* or most commonly known as the toilet make of dramatic statement in any powder room. If you want to add a bit of color to the outside of your commode or completely cover it with complex motifs give this decorating tip a try. For a complete matching ensemble don't neglect the pedestal sink, vanity, mirror and trash basket.

*Shower curtain liners* are less expensive that shower curtains but they are drab and boring. But not any more once you add your decorative images. (Don't worry your vinyl cut outs are water proof. See the FAQ section for more on that.)

Like the look of frosted glass then change a plain *shower surround* into a custom privacy enclosure. With the help of frosted or etched glass film you can do just that.

When guests come to visit you always have to tell them that the bathroom is the first door on the right, but when you *decorate your interior doors* with cute words like "Ladies & Gents" or "Water Closet" that eliminates the guess work.

Like the look of marble in the bathroom but don't want the hefty price tag of a stone slab? Take a garage sale find and turn that cheap *bathroom vanity* into a show piece by adding marble vinyl to the sink surround and backsplash.

**Bedroom**

*Glass blocks* come pre-drilled for LED lights and make great night lights or accent lights for any room. Use glass paints and stencil a design for a translucent glow.

Change the look of existing *wall paper* by stenciling repetitive shapes in a pattern or randomly. Give inexpensive wall coverings a custom high end look by adding painted accents.

If you make your own *accent pillows* you can change them often to fit the occasion. As a vacation reminder, a job promotion, well-earned retirement or make your own joke pillows with a funny pun.

What about *lamp shades*? You can apply any design you want to the outside of the shade to instantly dress it up and change the look but what about the reverse side. In the nineteenth century reverse painted lamps were all the rage.

These antiques are quite costly but you can create a similar look yourself. Apply you vinyl shapes to the underside of the shade. When the lamp is off you won't see the design but when the lamp is lit the shadow effect will look like a cool silhouette.

Did you grow up with those white roll down *window shades*? They are great for making the room dark but talk about dull and unattractive. You now have a blank canvas to decorate. If you want to try your hand at stenciling with paint, this would be a good project to try since the shades are cheap and easy to come by.

Personalize you guest room with *monogramed pillow cases*. In fancy hotels they leave chocolate candies on the pillows but when your guests retire they will see their name or initials on the pillow and feel right at home.

If you like the look of a *head board* and want the versatility of changing the look often use vinyl to create one on the wall above your bed. Geometric shapes are good for a modern style. Use asymmetrical designs with c-scrolls and shells for a French look. Go for a stained glass or glazed tile look if you want to reproduce the Mission or Arts and Craft style.

To add bits of romance to the bedroom apply vinyl letters to the wall quoting from your favorite love sonnet or poem.

If you like the classic look of gold leaf then turn any inexpensive *mirror* into an elegant show piece using metallic vinyl in gold, silver or copper. Their satin finish will reflect the light and add a satisficed look to your bedroom.

## Chapter Eleven - Personalized Gifts for Everyone on Your List

### Gifts for her

Some of these gift ideas can be decorated with painted stencils, craft vinyl or a little of both.

Create your own *designer shoes* by putting vinyl images on the soles of your high heel shoes. Give Nike a little competition and decorate your tennis shoes as well.

Change the look of *liquid soap or hand lotion dispenser* for each season of the year or to match your bathroom decor. They are inexpensive enough for you to change the look often.

Have you noticed how health-conscious we've become? Everywhere you look people are walking around with *plastic water bottles* but they don't have to be dull and boring. If you take yours to work no one will ever mistake it for theirs if it's decorated.

Wondering what to do with all those wedding pictures? Copy them on printable vinyl and turn them into a *wedding puzzle*. Instead of cutting the picture into the typical jigsaw pattern cut it into hearts, circles, squares and triangles.

Need wedding or anniversary gift ideas or just want to make something special for your powder room? Then try making *monogramed towel sets*.

Look for ceramic, glass or metal *figurines* that are mounted on a base which leaves you room to add an inspirational or funny sayings.

Turn your plain *umbrella* into a real head turner it will be easy to identify and you're sure to get a comment or two from anyone who sees it. They might even want you to make one for them.

Do you have a collection of cherished family recipes, if not why not contact your relatives and ask them for their tried and true recipes? Then make copies and send everyone that contributed their own collection of family recipes in a *storage box or binder* that you have beautifully decorated with food motifs.

Are you into scrapbooking? Why not collect photographs and memorabilia from relatives and create a scrapbook for them. You can decorate the album to match the theme of the scrapbook. You can also collect photographs from all your relatives making multiple copies of the photos and create a family archive to be sent to each family as a cherished *memory album.*

Here is an extra tip for all you family historians who save newspaper clippings of family achievements. To preserve the memories make sure you make photocopies of the clippings before they yellow and crumble. The acid in the newsprint will eventually destroy the article.

Daily planners are great for keeping us organized but they're not very stylish. Make sure to jazz up your *planner, diary or journal* and make the outside fun or whimsical while keeping your innermost thoughts safe and organized inside. Decorate them for yourself or customize them for gifts people will actually use and enjoy.

Whenever you give *gifts from your kitchen* make sure you decorate the container. That way your gift will look as good as it tastes.

Gone are the days of elegant twelve course dinner parties but if you still entertain in a formal way then decorate your *dinner napkins* and *table cloth* to capture a little elegance of those by gone days.

Do you or someone you know have a green thumb? Or if you're like me and have a brown thumb the only thing that ads beautiful color in my garden is the *flags and garden ornaments* that are covered in vinyl flowers and butterflies.

Instead of giving baby clothes as gifts surprise the new mother with an assortment of *baby products* like powder, shampoo, oil, lotion and wipes and of course decorate the containers. The hardest part will be deciding on which cute designs to choose from all the possibilities on the Cricut cartridges.

A *memorial of sympathy gift* is much appreciated during the grieving period. It shows your loving concern. A personalized item might include a framed picture, ceramic plate, figurine or a keychain.

Remember *family pets* with a garden flag where Fido is buried.

## Gifts for him

Leather bound books are expensive but with this idea you get the look of class with a twist. Have you heard of *altered books*? It's where you keep the book intact but hollow out a hidden compartment within the pages to hide something.

Reproduce your husband's favorite novel and decorate it with faux leather vinyl and keep it by his chair. You can store the TV remote in the hollowed out compartment that way everyone will know where to find the universal remote control.

Have you seen the price of those *sports jerseys*? You can save yourself a buck and customize his sweatshirt, hoodie, jacket and even the blanket he takes with him to the games. Just add his favorite team logo or the star players name and number to make any sports fan happy.

Turn your couch potato into a weekend athlete with custom gear. Personalize any *sports equipment* with inspirational cheers like Winners Make It Happen or Don't Sit Get Fit. When you decorate his skies, snow board, golf bag, tennis racket cover or jogging shoes you're showing your support.

Been to the airport recently and noticed how everybody's luggage looks the same? Make his luggage easy to identify with the design that's near and dear to his heart. If decorating his luggage is a bit over the top then create *luggage tags* that are easy to spot.

If he likes the idea of making his belongings easy to spot then don't forget his *laptop, tablet and phone.*

Instead of a gift basket fill a *coffee mug* with goodies on the inside while making the outside good enough to eat with sweet treats like cookies, cupcakes or pie alamode.

Do you have a gardener, chief, artist or photographer in the family? Just match up his interest with a book on the same subject and make a vinyl *dust jacket and a bookmark* you're sure to make him smile when he receives your thoughtful handmade gift.

Children are always looking for handmade gift items for dad. They can embellish existing items like *wallets, mousepads or neckties.*

Give the man in your life an award. There are dozens of *desk top plaques* that you can add a photo and vinyl lettering to. Let everyone know he's the world's greatest husband.

Home brewing and wine making have become popular hobbies. Give the brew master in your life a personalized *beer mug, stein or a set of wine glasses.*

Honor the master griller in your home and decorate a *chef's apron* and *hat* with barbecue designs.

Using exterior vinyl you can customize *license plate frames* to say just about anything. Do a search for license plate frame sayings if you need ideas.

Dress up inexpensive glass, wood or metal boxes into *dazzling jewelry boxes*. If he's always looking for his keys and wants a place to store loose change then these decorated boxes are made to order.

Is there a card shark on your list? Decorative wall *plaques, drink costars* and *gaming chips* can be personalized to say Rick's Casino or Bill's Poker Palace.

If you're lucky enough to have your very own grease monkey or handy man *brighten up the garage or basement* workshop with a sign that says Mechanic On Duty All Night or You Break It I Fix It.

**Gifts for kids**

Be everyone's favorite mom with this gift idea. If your child is on a team decorate inexpensive *sports bottles* in the teams colors picturing the mascot or team name and personalize them for each member. Don't forget the coach.

Do you coach little league or soccer and haven't found a sponsor to buy those expensive uniforms? *T-shirts and baseball caps* can be decorated with team colors and kids names for a lot less than professional uniforms now that you know how to use iron on vinyl.

For all you homeschoolers now you can create *honor student bumper stickers*. They usually say something like "Proud Parents of an Outstanding Student at Home School USA."

*Personalized key chains* make nice teacher gifts but don't stop there travel mugs or water bottles would be appreciated too.

Does your *kid's backpack* have a way of disappearing? If so make your child's bag personable so it's stands out and no one can mistake it for their own. In fact you can put your child's name on just about any clothing item shoes too. Depending on the item you can make small labels with adhesive vinyl for the inside of shoes for example and soft iron on vinyl that feels good to wear on clothing.

If you have a hard time getting your youngsters to bed at night try decorating their *pajamas and night gowns* with Disney characters, their favorite animal or play time motifs so they want to get ready for bed.

Make bedtime fun and educational by *decorating the ceiling* with glow-in-the-dark vinyl stars, planets and our solar system.

Make mealtime fun for those picky eaters by decorating their *glasses, plates, bowls* and *placemats* with jokes, riddles or funny sayings.

It's never too late to teach your children how to cook. Give them incentive to learn by putting their name on an *apron, oven mitts and potholders* and encourage them to join you in the kitchen.

Instead of those plain plastic containers help your children clean up their room and let them choose the designs shapes and characters to decorate their *storage bins*. This would be a good beginner project that even children could do. Just make sure your designs are small and simple. Since these are just like decals or stickers all they have to do is peel and stick it to the storage container.

If you're good with tools and have a hand held or table top jigsaw then you can create your own *stenciled wooden puzzles*. There are a bunch of patterns available from baby puzzles with simple cut out images like the alphabet or numbers to 3-D dimensional puzzles of buildings, animals and brain teasers. Remember vinyl doesn't stick well to raw wood.

Don't want to use power tools but like the idea a making puzzles. Try this suggestion. Turn any *photograph, clip art or vector image* into a puzzle. Just use the printable vinyl to copy your image and cut the image into puzzle pieces.

You can also *embellish existing puzzles* like the Rubik's cube. Think of a theme for your puzzle using any Cricut cartridge to cut out the vinyl pieces small enough to fit on the squares of the cube.

If you like to sew personalize stuffed animals and teddy bears with doll clothes. You can even start your own line of *personalized doll clothes*. Your customer would send you a picture of their little girl wearing her favorite outfit and you would recreate it for her doll. That way they can dress the same and be like twins.

Make personalized doll lookalikes with printable vinyl. Just copy the child's photograph and turn them into *paper dolls* for girls and *action figures* for boys.

Kids love bright colors so use fluorescent or glitter vinyl and turn inexpensive boxes into *treasure chests* so they have a secret place to hide their favorite keepsakes.

Create your own *travel games* and keep kids entertained in the car. Save your cookie and popcorn tin's to store the game pieces and use the lid as you're playing surface or you can use a metal tray as the game board. Use magnetic vinyl to cut out the game pieces for tic-tac-toe, checkers, chess and memory games.

If you have the 50 states Cricut cartridge you can use it to cut out the states and help your children *learn geography*. If you don't have that cartridge here's what you can do.

All you need is an inkjet printer, a map of the United States, printable magnetic vinyl and scissors. Just print out the map and cut each state out with scissors.

# Chapter Twelve - Money Making Ideas

Making money with your crafts is not as hard as you might think. First decide whether you want to start a small business or you just want your hobby to pay for itself.

You can run a craft business from your own home without investing in office or retail space. You choose your own hours and types of projects you want to produce. It's a chance to use your creativity and also make extra money.

## Things to consider before starting your craft business

There are always legalities to consider when starting any business. They change from state to state and even from city to city. So you'll need to check online for your local laws. You may need to obtain a local license or file for a fictitious name certificate. This shows you're doing business as (DBA) Sally's Crafts or Alice's Craft Emporium.

In the beginning you can probably work as a sole proprietor and won't need to incorporate. You'll file a Schedule C with your personal tax return.

You'll need to track your income and expenses carefully. You will be responsible for paying taxes on the money you earn. But you only need to pay tax on the profits. You can subtract the money you spend on materials and equipment.

Remember: self-employment tax is higher than the tax rate you pay as an employee. Put money aside so you'll have it when taxes are due. You may need to set up quarterly tax payments to avoid penalties. Talking to an accountant is always a good idea since the tax laws change.

To start with you may want to track your income and expenses on a spread sheet. But when possible invest in software such as Quicken. This will make your job much easier. Plus you can print out reports to take to your accountant once a year. This will decrease his fees since he'll have less work to do.

Starting a sideline business can be time consuming. It's best if you can get your family on board from the beginning. Let them know how the extra money will take stress off the family budget or maybe help pay for a special vacation. If your family knows what you're working towards they'll be more excited about helping you. Teenagers may be able to work in the business with you and learn valuable skills.

**Establish your brand**

One reason why Etsy is so popular is they pride themselves in bringing artists and customers together to develop a relationship. So it's your job to tell people who you are and why they should buy from you.

To build your credibility post videos on YouTube that explain the process you use to create crafts. This helps brand you as an expert. Plus, even though viewers might like to learn to do the projects themselves; they often decide it's not worth the time and effort and will click through to purchase from your website.

Always link back to your main website or craft store from your social media sites. Set up your signature to include your business contact information when posting to online forums and in your email.

Keep your business name in front of your customers and make it easy for them to find you. Include a business card or refrigerator magnet with your company info on it with every new order. Include an extra business card and ask them to hand it to a friend.

**The customer is always right.**

Always offer good customer service. If someone emails you with a question get back to them as soon as possible.

Package and ship your products carefully. Make sure you add enough to your shipping costs to allow for postage and packaging. You may want to offer gift wrapping for an extra charge.

Ask for feedback. It's the best way to find out how to improve your service. Make it easy for customers to leave testimonials on your webpage. A happy customer goes a long way in building your credibility.

State your return or refund policy clearly on your website so there are no surprises for your customers.

Creating projects with your Circuit can be more than just a fun hobby. If you're willing to put in the effort you can build a sideline or even a full-time business while doing something you love.

## How to price your products

When deciding how to price your products consider the following costs:

Price of material
Your time
Business expenses for advertising and website hosting
Time you spend marketing your business
Packing materials
Shipping costs

Many crafters devalue their time. Decide how much you want to make per hour. Then determine how much time each project takes you to complete. Add your time into the equation. Otherwise you'll burn out fast and won't make much of a profit.

While you can start your prices on the low end and then raise them; this can be harder than anticipated. It's better to start your prices at a rate that gives you a decent profit margin. Take the best photos possible of your projects. Write compelling descriptions how the customer will benefit from owing your item. Also give exact dimensions and specific details proving your projects are worth top dollar.

When marketing your crafts; always be aware of upcoming holidays. Mark your calendar so your projects are ready in plenty of time for holiday shoppers.

You may think that after Christmas all online shopping ceases for a while. But January is usually the second busiest month of the year. So take advantage of the shopping mentality and get your items in front of hungry buyers.

Remember to create projects for personal holiday such as:

Anniversaries
Baby births
Graduations
House warming
New Job
Promotions
Retirement
Weddings

People are always celebrating something. Create projects based on special occasions.

Offering personalization can be a huge marketing advantage and can apply to any item like wine glasses, decorative wall hangings or sports teams, these items are considered of greater value if they've been custom ordered and made specifically for the buyer using their initials or child's name.

Don't make a large quantity of one item until you see if it will sell. This is the beauty of an online business. You can always test new projects on a small basis instead of having boxes of unsold items sitting in your garage.

Use sites like eBay and Etsy to do market research. See what's selling and what not to waste your time on creating. Look for hot items and improve on them by adding your own personal touch.

When you find a popular item that sells well then get busy and make more.

During peak seasons you might want to hire additional help. Your own kids are a good starting place, or maybe your friends. You can probably find a few moms who would like to earn some extra cash while their children are at school.

You can show them step by step how to create the products so you're sure there is no loss of quality.

Or you can have them handle the packing of the items or they can help you keep track of your expenses and income by entering information on your computer. It's easy to get behind on these types of mundane tasks. You can often make more money by producing more crafts to sell and outsourcing the day to day details of your business. They can also help answer emails. This frees your time to do what you do best.

**How will you sell your crafts?**

Before starting your craft business decide if you want to sell offline, online or both. Do you want to specialize or sell a little of everything? Are you a people person and enjoy the interaction with local customers or do you prefer the anonymity the Internet offers? The more you know about your business the easier it will be to reach your goals.

Selling online allows you to broaden your market worldwide or at least country wide. You may or may not want to ship to other countries.

You can set up a website fairly inexpensively yourself and incorporate shopping cart technology or use PayPal buttons.

If you decide to go with one of the online marketplaces they will let you build and host your store for free or my charge a monthly membership. I have listed dozens of craft sites later in this chapter where you can set up shop.

Networking with other people can help you get the word out about your business. LinkedIn and other business networking sites like Efactor, Ryze and Startupnation are places you can look for likeminded individuals who can help you.

If you find a person who knows about advertising exchange services, he launches your advertising campaign in exchange for personalized gifts for his family.

Don't forget to set up your free page on Facebook that links to your website and interact with other crafters and small business owners. There are apps that will connect your store to your Facebook page so you can post and show off your creativity. Just do a search for them.

Whatever social media sites you frequent remember to mention your business and of course pin photos of your creations on Pinterest.

**Where to sell crafts online.**

Don't forget to do your research and see what's already selling online like stick figure families that display on car windows, personalized gift items for every occasion, clothing of all kinds not just T-shirts and hats, refrigerator magnets for clubs, organizations, business as well as individuals or go green with grocery tote bags, really if there is a market for it find a way of cashing in on it by adding your own personal touch.

Before you sign up with any online store visit their forums to learn what buyers and sellers say about the community. Are they happy with the site or is there need for improvement. Some let you build your store for free but charge a listing fee or a monthly membership. Do your homework and find the best marketplace that suites your needs.

Here is a list of online marketplaces where you can sell your handmade creations.

**Aftcra.com** only sells Made in America handmade products. There are no listing fees for your items.

**ArtFire.com** is a marketplace where crafter's and buyers come together from around the world to buy, sell and interact. They have an active support forum.

**Azcraze.com** has no listing fees or commissions just a small monthly fee to list unlimited items.

**Bigcartel.com** gives artists a helping hand creating on online store and running a creative business.

**Bonanza.com** claims sellers prefer their site over eBay and Amazon for its ease of use.

**Craftisart.com** is an artesian marketplace with no listing fees just a monthly or yearly membership.

**Custommade.com** lets buyers post a custom order that you are willing to fill.

**eBay.com** of course needs no introduction.

**Esty.com** is another well-known market center. Their forums and online guides help you set up shop.

**eCater.com** offers a free web store builder as well as an online marketplace.

**Ezebee.com** is a small business network and marketplace where you can even post classified ads.

**Festivalnet.com** lists art and craft shows, street fairs and music festivals which are all fun places to show off your creations. You can search the site by state or month and find more than 26,000 listings.

**FreeCraftFair.com** is more of a directory offering low-cost advertising options on their site that gets thousands of unique visitors each month.

**Glccraftmall.com** has a try before you buy option that lets you open a craft shop and list 12 items free.

**Handmadeartists.com** helps promote their members with free advertising. There are no fees or dues to be a forum member. To set up a shop they require a membership fee.

**Icraftgifts.com** specializes in handmade items and allows you to import listings from eBay and Etsy into your easy to set up storefront.

**Imadeitmarket.com** organizes craft events and is always looking for sellers to exhibit their creations.

**Localharvest.org** farmers markets often sell booth space to crafters. Search the site to see if there is a market in your area.

**Luulla.com** is an online marketplace for small businesses. They feature and help promote your creations on Facebook, Twitter and Pinterest.

**Makerfaire.com** lists family-friendly festivals earth wide where creative people come together to buy and sell homemade items.

**Shophandmade.com** is now offering a free store for you to sell your craft items.

**Silkfair.com** offers a simple store option as well as a custom storefront.

**Storenvy.com** is a fast growing social shopping marketplace that helps you set up shop in minutes.

**Spoonflower.com** is for all your designers out there. Just upload an image and create fabric, wallpaper or wrapping paper

**Supermarkethq.com** connects artists, designers and entrepreneurs with customers.

**Thecraftstar.com** is a unique boutique of handmade items where you can list for free but pay a membership fee.

**Tosouk.com** is based in the UK and says it's a free place to list your crafts for sale.

**Unisquare.com** claim to fame is that it offers auctions without any listing fees. Storefronts are available too.

**Zibbet.com** offers a free, starter or pro option when using their site.

For those of you who want to see how they sell crafts across the pond check out these other UK based sites.

**Ccoriandr.com**

**Creativestores.co.uk**

**Folksy.com**

**Misi.co.uk**

I wish I could add Amazon.com to this list but for now they require that items sold on their site have a UPC or bar code. You can buy bar codes but that would cut into your profit margin unless you sell high end items. Perhaps they will change this requirement at some future date.

**Where to sell crafts offline**

Get in the habit of carrying business cards and flyers with you wherever you go there is always an opportunity to hand someone a card or post a flyer on a community information board.

With the advent of desktop publishing you can print your own or visit Vistaprint.com and order 500 business cards for 10 bucks.

Your top priority is to get the word out and let people know you are open for business and ready to take orders. One way to enlist the help of family, friends and workmates is to give them one of your products as a free gift. If they love it they can't help but tell other people about your craft items don't forget your kid's teachers too.

Offer a referral program either a discount or a free item when someone refers a customer to generate business.

Make sure to advertise your business on your vehicle now that you know how to apply vinyl letters to car windows or create a magnetic sign for the car door.

Visit local stores in your community and ask them if you can display your business cards or flyers.

Often times sign shops are not willing to do small jobs but are happy to refer people to you so leave your contact info with them.

Think of complementary businesses such as photographers, bakeries, caterers, florists, wedding planners, limousine services and bridal shops who deal with customers planning special events like weddings, anniversaries, family reunions or retirement parties. These are the type of customers that would be interested in personalized gift items you create. Leave them your cards and perhaps they'll recommend you to their clients.

You can rent a craft booth at antique malls if there are consignment stores in your area check them out as well.
Once you have an inventory of products you can set up a booth at swap meets, farmers markets, craft shows even art and music festivals.

Visit **localharvest.org** to find farmers markets listings in your area or search **festivalnet.com/indexes.html** for craft fairs, music festivals and street fairs.

Make sure you know of any community events scheduled in your area as you may be able to set up a display as well. Put on a decorating workshop at a community center and show people how to use vinyl. These how-to workshops are a fun way to generate business.

Set up a table in front of your local supermarket and take advantage of the foot traffic.

You may even consider doing home parties.

Seek out charitable organizations and fundraising events to set up shop donating part of your proceeds to charity.

Is this all the information you need to know to start a craft business? Obviously not but it's enough information to help you make an educated decision. There are endless online guides, video tutorials and even library books that give detailed information on how to start a home-based business.

# Chapter Thirteen - 101 Inspirational Wallies

Now that you know how to apply vinyl letters to walls here are 101 quotes to choose from. Some will inspire you to be the best you can be while others will motivate you to live a happier life and to succeed at work or play. Still others will move you to make the most of your relationships with family and friends.

And some of these wacky words of wisdom are flat out funny bringing a smile to your face whenever you read them on your living room, bedroom, home office or kitchen walls.

1. A dream is not something that you wake up from, but something that wakes you up.
2. A goal is a dream with a deadline.
3. A house without books is like a room without windows.
4. A kind smile and a pure heart will win over others from the start.
5. A man is but the product of his thoughts what he thinks, he becomes.
6. A short hug is sometimes better than a long talk.
7. A successful man is one who makes more money than his wife can spend.
8. A successful marriage requires falling in love many times, always with the same person.
9. Adolescence and snow are problems that disappear when ignored long enough.
10. Adults are just kids grown up.
11. After all... tomorrow is another day.

12. Age is an issue of mind over matter. If you don't mind, it doesn't matter.
13. Animals are my friends...and I don't eat my friends.
14. Any idiot can face a crisis—its day to day living that wears you out.
15. Being away is fine, but being at home is best.
16. Business opportunities are like buses, there's always another one coming.
17. Chains of habit are too light to be felt until they are too heavy to be broken.
18. Depth of friendship does not depend on length of acquaintance.
19. Don't limit your challenges; challenge your limits.
20. Dream and give yourself permission to envision the person you choose to be.
21. Dreams transform into thoughts and thoughts result in action.
22. Drive your business. Let not your business drive you.
23. Every great business is built on friendship.
24. Every time you tell a lie, a bit of truth must die.
25. Everyone thinks of changing the world, but no one thinks of changing himself.
26. Everything has beauty, but not everyone sees it.
27. Everything is funny as long as it is happening to somebody else.
28. Failure is simply an opportunity to begin again, this time more intelligently.
29. Good coffee is a pleasure - good friends are a treasure.
30. Hate the sin and love the sinner.

31. Sometimes we put walls up not to keep people out, but to see who cares enough to break them down.

32. Humor is a rubber sword - it allows you to make a point without drawing blood.

33. I don't mind living in a man's world, as long as I can be a woman in it.

34. I drink to make other people more interesting.

35. I have no country to fight for; my country is the earth; I am a citizen of the world.

36. I like work: it fascinates me. I can sit and look at it for hours.

37. If we couldn't laugh we would all go insane.

38. If you can't believe it, you can't achieve it.

39. If you don't love yourself, how do you expect anybody else to?

40. If you tell the truth, you don't have to remember the lies.

41. If you want breakfast in bed, sleep in the kitchen.

42. If you're gonna be two-faced at least make one of them pretty.

43. Imagination means nothing without doing.

44. In order to succeed, your desire for success should be greater than your fear of failure.

45. Is the glass half full, or half empty? It depends on whether you're pouring, or drinking.

46. It's never too late to become what you might have been.

47. Just remember, when you're over the hill, you pick up speed.

48. Life is really simple, but we insist on making it complicated.

49. Live as if you were to die tomorrow. Learn as if you were to live forever.

50. Love is an irresistible desire to be irresistibly desired.

51. Love, laughter and friendships are always welcome here.

52. May all who enter as guests, leave our home as friends.

53. May you always have love to share, health to spare, and friends that care.

54. Music is the wine that fills the cup of silence.

55. Never invest more than you can walk away from.

56. Never judge a book by its movie.

57. No dreamer is ever too small; no dream is ever too big.

58. Nothing is so necessary for a young man as the company of intelligent women.

59. One good thing about music, when it hits you, you feel no pain.

60. Only the wisest and stupidest of men never change.

61. Our family tree is full of nuts.

62. Pain is temporary quitting lasts forever.

63. Parents are not interested in justice; they're interested in peace and quiet.

64. People become successful the minute they decide to.

65. Pets are not our whole life, but they make our lives whole.

66. Remember that silence is sometimes the best answer.

67. Remember, if you want a different result, do something different.

68. Rule No.1: Never lose hope. Rule No.2: Never forget rule No.1.

69. Strangers are just friends I haven't met yet.
70. The afternoon knows what the morning never suspected.
71. The best sermons are lived, not preached.
72. The best way to find yourself is to lose yourself in the service of others.
73. The dictionary is the only place where success comes before work.
74. The future belongs to those who believe in the beauty of their dreams.
75. The greater the obstacle, the more glory in achieving it.
76. The greatness of a nation can be judged by the way its animals are treated.
77. The less people know, the more stubbornly they know it.
78. The only people to get even with are those who have helped you.
79. The only way to avoid housework is to live outside.
80. The past is a ghost, the future a dream and all we ever have is now.
81. The secret of business is to know something that nobody else knows.
82. The worst-mistake is to be afraid of making one.
83. Think before you speak. Read before you think.
84. This kitchen is closed due to illness; I'm sick of cooking.
85. Those who cannot change their minds cannot change anything.
86. To be a champion, you have to believe in yourself when nobody else will.

87. To get the full value of joy you must have somebody to share it with.

88. True love doesn't have a happy ending, because true love never ends.

89. Wanting to be someone else is a waste of the person you are.

90. We are not promised tomorrow so make the most of today.

91. Whatever you choose to do, choose to do it well.

92. When a man murders a tiger he calls it sport; when a tiger kills him he calls it ferocity.

93. When anger rises, think of the consequences.

94. When searching for direction, the only way to look is up.

95. Worry is like rocking a chair; it gives you something to do, but gets you nowhere.

96. You are never too old to set another goal or to dream a new dream.

97. You cannot open a book without learning something.

98. You cannot run and hide from yourself.

99. You don't stop laughing when you grow old; you grow old when you stop laughing.

100. You will do foolish things, but do them with enthusiasm.

101. Your attitude, not your aptitude, will determine your altitude.

# Chapter Fourteen - Video Tutorials

YouTube is a great resource for how to videos. I use it all the time when I want to learn something new or fix a problem.

For you visual learners these simple tutorials will show you what you need to know in step by step instructions.

### Cutting Vinyl Basics
If you have not cut vinyl before here is a basic run thru demonstrating how to cut it, use transfer tape and apply your design.
https://youtu.be/uLPCNCTXzrg

### Wall Art Applications
Here's how to apply wall art. These are short simple videos that show you the different methods of applying vinyl lettering.
https://youtu.be/cEAIJevzz9Q?list=PLF207566E73AB933F

### Car Window Installation Tips
This video shows you how to fix problems when applying stickers to car windows.
https://youtu.be/6ZvahnkLJOM

### Removing Frosted Vinyl
Avoid the nightmare of removing frosted vinyl from glass by using these tips.
https://youtu.be/vqI2nEj1vo4

## Wet Method For Car Windows

Use the wet method when applying vinyl letters to the outside of your car window. Remember if you're applying the words to the inside of your window they have to be spelled backwards and then flipped. Otherwise your lettering will be backwards and unreadable.

https://youtu.be/PO9iNQV-hYE

## Armour Etch Tip

Want better results when using glass etching cream?

https://youtu.be/AO2qNxalupQ

## T-shirt Vinyl Help

Working with heat transfer vinyl for cloth applications is easy once you know how.

https://youtu.be/r-o46JcoRgA

## Glass Cutting 101

Give plain wine bottles real aesthetic value. Learn how to cut glass the right way for your etching, stenciling or vinyl projects.

https://youtu.be/sFXngPx3w3M

## Make Your Own Glass Cutter

You can either buy a glass cutter of build one yourself.

https://youtu.be/6tNgJKQCl7k

## Cheap Sand Blasting Kit

Love the look of sand blasted etched glass but don't want to buy expensive equipment?

http://www.youtube.com/watch?v=eVFji6cQO5Q

# Chapter Fifteen FAQ'S

In this last chapter I want to address the questions I most often hear when working with vinyl and glass etching projects.

**Vinyl FAQS**

**1. Where can I buy vinyl?** Local craft stores often stock vinyl. I haven't had as much luck with local stores. I don't know if it's just a cheaper type of vinyl they sell or if they keep it in stock too long. You may have a different experience. There are endless online sources available as well or work out a deal with a local sign shop.

**2. Is Cricut vinyl my only option?** No. There are several manufacturers of craft vinyl on the market. Cricut vinyl is made by Oracal but here are other brand names to check out like Avery, Arlon, Creative Film, Endura, FDC, Green Star, GT5, LVG InterCal, Mactac, Siser, Transvinyl Flexx, VinylEase, Vector and 3M.

**3. What settings should I use for cutting?** I find setting the blade at 3, pressure at 3 and speed at 3 works well for me. But you'll need to adjust for different vinyl since it's not all the same thickness. Also, for most projects you'll want a light "kiss cut" that cuts the vinyl and not the backing. But for reusable stencils you need the cut to go all the way through the backing so you'll need a deeper cut.

**4. Can I cut vinyl on my Cricut without using a mat?** No.

Always use a mat just like you do when cutting paper do not remove the backing just place the vinyl on the mat paper side down.

**5. Will vinyl stick to any surface?** Almost, for best results avoid these surfaces brick, cement, greasy walls, leather, raw wood, stucco, unpainted metal and old peeling paint. If you're working outdoors avoid applying vinyl in hot and cold weather. For successful applications the temperature should be between 60 and 80 degrees Fahrenheit.

**6. What type of projects should I start with?** If you never worked with vinyl before start with projects with removable static cling vinyl. It is more forgiving when placing it on a surface and can be readjusted easily.  Also, use a pattern that doesn't have a lot of intricate details. This lowers the risk of tearing the design when weeding it and attaching it to its final surface. Printable vinyl is also a good starter project.

**7. Can vinyl get wet?** Yes. It is not going to hurt your vinyl if it gets wet. However, the type of vinyl determines how water resistant it is. Vinyl made for outdoor signs is more water resistant and can also stand up to the sun's UV rays longer without fading, cracking or curling.

**8. Are vinyl decals dish washer safe?** Yes. Just use exterior vinyl like Oracal 651 or 751 and adjust the temperature settings avoiding high temperature wash and rinse cycles. Eventually your decals will curl. Hand washing will extend the life of your vinyl creations.

**9. Can vinyl be removed later?** Yes. The longer the vinyl has been attached to a surface and the more direct sunlight hits the vinyl; the greater chance of leaving residue. Glass cleaners work well for removing residue from car windows and other glass surfaces without damage. Painted walls can suffer damage when the vinyl is removed if it has been in place for a long period of time; usually three years or more.

**10. How can I save money when buying vinyl?** Talk to local sign shops and see if they'll give you their scraps or sell them to you cheaply. They may also be willing to sell you pieces of vinyl that they buy on large rolls. Otherwise, you'll need to compare prices from vendors and search for the best prices. Buy in small quantities until you're sure the company is selling the type of vinyl you're happy with. Cheap vinyl can pucker or peel off quickly. You don't want to waste your time and effort producing projects that are quickly ruined because of poor quality vinyl.

**11. How long can I store vinyl?** I prefer to use vinyl within two years. If I'm not going to use it right away I store it in airtight plastic containers so it doesn't get dusty. The tricky thing is; you don't know how old the vinyl is when you buy it. If you store it too long the adhesive can lose its effectiveness. So I suggest not buying in bulk unless you know you're going to be making a lot of vinyl projects.

**12. Is it necessary to seal or add a topcoat to vinyl?** No. But you may like the look a topcoat or glaze adds to the finished product. When choosing a clear polyurethane avoid solvent and oil-based products. Look for a water-based clear coat that you brush on. Some aerosol products will cause the decal to lift or curl. Mod Podge is also an option.

**13. What if my vinyl refuses to cut properly?** Adjust your setting slightly up or down depending on whether the cut is too deep or too shallow. Make sure your blades are sharp and clean use a Q-tip and alcohol to remove any sticky residue. Use a new mat when cutting vinyl.

**14. When do I use application sprays?** If you're working with frosted vinyl, large windows or mirrors due yourself a favor and use an application fluid. Exterior applications in colder weather will perform better when you use the liquid method as well.

**15. Will anything get rid of ghosting on chalkboard vinyl?** Yes. Regular chalk and Bistro chalk markers will leave a residue behind because of the coarse texture of the vinyl. Try using a Mr. Clean magic eraser for best results.

**16. Is there any iron on vinyl for nylon and leather?** Yes. Most heat transfer vinyl works well on cotton and polyester fabric but Siser Easyweed Extra and ThermoFlex Xtra can be applied to leather and nylon items.

**17. Why won't the backing paper peel off?** If you cut the vinyl too deep some of the adhesive can ooze out and stick to the backing making it had to weed and remove. Here are some suggestions. Try heating the decal by setting it in direct sunlight for ten minutes. Iron the backing for ten seconds with an iron set on low or pop it into a microwave oven for three seconds. Heating the glue helps the vinyl to let go of the release liner.

**18. If vinyl sticks to itself is the design ruined?** No. If you removed the backing paper and the letters stick to themselves squirt them with a little application fluid and gently pull them apart.

**Glass Etching FAQS**

**1. Is glass etching permanent?** Yes. Once the glass is etched it can't be removed. So cover all the surfaces of a project carefully so none of the wrong areas are exposed to the etching cream.

**2. What kind of glass can be etched?** Both clear and colored glass can be etched. You can use etching to make inexpensive glass items look more decorative. Get in the habit of looking at existing glass objects that you can enhance by etching.

**3. Is glass the only surface I can etch?** No. Ceramic, porcelain, marble, slate and mirrors can be etched.

**4. Can Pyrex dishes be etched?** Yes and no. Some glass contains lead or plastic which interfere with the etching process. Test a small area to be sure you'll get the result you want. Do not try to etch over a logo or design already in the glass.

**5. Is it hard to etch rounded surfaces like wine glasses?** It can be. Don't use a large design that goes all the way around the glass. Be patient when applying the stencil. Make small slits in the stencil to assure it wraps around the glass properly. You need to be sure all the edges are secured or etching cream will get under the stencil and ruin your design.

**6. Is it safe to eat off dishes that have been etched?** Yes. They are dishwasher safe and do not require any type of sealant or topcoat.

**7. Can etching cream be reused?** Some brands can. You can simply scrape off the cream and put it back in its container. Read the directions carefully to know if the cream you're using can be reused.

**8. Is etching cream dangerous?** Not if used correctly and the directions are carefully followed. But it is acidic and can be dangerous if not used the right way. Breathing the fumes is not a good idea so always work in a well-ventilated area and wear gloves for added protection. Keep it away from children and pets. Remember the save your sink and the environment tip in chapter 5.

**9. Can I leave etching cream on longer for better results?** Yes. Twenty minutes is the longest I've tried. Armour Etch contains sulfuric acid. You run the risk of damaging the stencil and ruining the design if you leave it on much longer. The caustic ingredient in Etchall is ammonium bifluoride and can be left on for an hour if you want.

**10. Etching cream sounds too dangerous since I have small children in my home. Is there another way I can**

**create that frosted glass look?** You can use a stencil and frosted spray paint. Or you can use frosted vinyl. The design will be placed on top of the glass instead of etched permanently into it.

**11. Will food stain etched designs?** Yes. So always etch the back of glass plates and dishes unless they are for decorative purposes only.

**12. Will etching cream frost large glass areas?** Not very well. For solid etching use an etching dip or bath and dunk the glass into the liquid for a frosted effect.

**13. Do I have to use a stencil when etching glass?** No. You can freehand your design. Just use a paint brush and paint on the etching cream.

**14. Is there anything I can do to enhance the image and make it really stand out?** Yes. Do a search for metallic wax like Rub n Buff and apply a little white to the design. You can also use glass paints.

## Concluding words of encouragement

Craft vinyl adds a whole new array of projects you can create with your Cricut machine. Don't be dismayed with the learning process. Once you've mastered the basic techniques your imagination will go wild with possibilities.

I hope this book will guide you through the basics and eliminate a lot of the problems I encountered along the way.

Whether you're making T-shirts for your son's rock band, animal décor for your granddaughter's crib or personalized engraved wine glasses; vinyl projects are fun, practical and beautiful.

Plus, you may be able to make some extra money by selling your creations.

Don't limit the possibilities. Use your imagination and get started today.

Enjoy!

*Maryann Gillespie*

# About the Author

I got in the habit of looking for quick solutions to all those annoying problems I had as a beginner working with craft vinyl. Now it's one of my most favorite things to cut on my Cricut machine. I've done a ton of research and gathered what I feel are valuable tips and decorating ideas for every room.

So I got to thinking if these tips, tricks and troubleshooting solutions have helped me, maybe they will help other Cricuter's. If you've seen the forums you know Cricut crafters are generous, love to share and are more than willing to help, ergo the reason I wrote this handy guide and my first Cricut Tips book.

Have you found any of these tips useful? If so please help me get the word out. Mention this craft vinyl book on your blog, tweet about it or post it on your Facebook page.

Thanks for your help and happy crafting.

# Notes

Made in the USA
San Bernardino, CA
27 March 2016